A TREASURY OF CLASSIC RECIPES FOR APPETIZERS, SOUPS, SALADS AND DESSERTS

by
Michelle A. Preston

TABLE OF CONTENTS

INTRODUCTION

Whether you're serving a dinner for a family of four, or planning an elaborate party, knowing a repertoire of appetizers, soups, salads, and desserts can only enhance your cooking plans. In her *A Treasury Of Classic Appetizers, Soups, Salads And Desserts*, Michelle A. Preston offers a host of recipes that will help you successfully round out any menu, no matter how simple or elaborate it may be.

In *Appetizers*, the first section of the book, Mrs. Preston includes a variety of beginning courses. There are appetizers that can be served alone at a cocktail party, appetizers that provide an introduction to the heavy meal to come, and hearty appetizers that can provide the bulk of a light meal. Always remember that appetizers should play the role of the "enticer," and should never completely stunt the diner's hunger. Also, presentation can play a large role in the success of any appetizer. Hint: try serving appetizers in the living room! You'll find yourself with more room at the dinner table, as well as whetting everyone's appetite for the delicious meal to come.

Next up is the *Soups* chapter, in which Mrs. Preston suggests recipes which can be used for a light lunch, a full meal, or as a delicious alternative for the second (or third if you prefer your salad before your soup) course. Always remember to use only the freshest of ingredients, and to have patience! Many soups take several hours to cook in order to bring out their fullest flavor. An economical favorite, soups are a cooking tradition.

In the following *Salads* section, Mrs. Preston includes a salad for everyone, including fruit, fish, egg, and garden salads. Low in fat and high in nutritional value, salads go great with almost any meal. As with the soups, always use the freshest greens available when putting together a salad. And remember, salads can also be served *after* your main course as an attractive refresher.

The final portion of the book, *Desserts*, offers luscious creations from Mrs. Preston's kitchen. While not always low in calories, these delicious sweets will prove a hit with any hungry eater.

APPETIZERS

Mexican Quesadillas

½ pound Monterey Jack cheese, grated
1 can green chilis, seeded, pitted, and shredded
8 corn tortillas

1) Place two tablespoons of cheese and a few pieces of chili in the center of each tortilla and fold in half. Fasten with a toothpick.

2) Bake the tortillas at 400 degrees for 8 to 10 minutes.

Serves 8

Sour Cream Dip for Vegetables

1 cup sour cream
½ cup Miracle Whip
1 tablespoon seasoning salt

1) Blend well. Use carrot sticks, celery sticks, cucumber slices, cauliflower florets, or any raw vegetable you can dip.

Pearl Crabtree
Montesuma, IN

Hot and Spicy Egg Spread

12 hard boiled eggs, peeled and chopped
½ cup butter
3 teaspoons Worcestershire sauce
3 teaspoons celery seed
3 tablespoons parsley, chopped
¼ teaspoon red pepper
1 teaspoon salt

1) Mix the eggs and butter together until smooth and creamy.

2) Add the Worcestershire sauce, celery seed, parsley, red pepper, and salt. Mix well.

Serves 12

Chicken Nuggets with Herbs

1 chicken breast, skinned and boned
⅛ cup bread crumbs
⅛ cup grated Parmesan cheese
¼ teaspoon salt
¼ teaspoon thyme
½ teaspoon basil
⅛ cup butter, melted

1) Cut the chicken breast into small, bite sized pieces.

2) Combine the remaining ingredients with the exception of the butter.

3) Dip the pieces of chicken in melted butter, then coat in the herb mixture. Place in a baking pan and bake in a 425 degree oven for 10 minutes.

Serves 10

Fun Cheese Party Dip

½ pound cream cheese
2½ cups sour cream
1 onion, diced
4 tablespoons pineapple juice
4 teaspoons Worcestershire sauce

1) Mix all of the ingredients together until rich and creamy. Chill before serving.

Serves 10

Cream Cheese Dip

16 ounces of soft cream cheese
1 cup plain yogurt
1 teaspoon salt
¼ teaspoon dill weed

1) Beat the ingredients together until rich and creamy.

Serves 6

Mexican Guacamole

2 medium tomatoes, peeled and crushed
4 avocados, halved, pitted, peeled, and crushed
4 tablespoons chili peppers, chopped
½ cup onion, chopped
3 tablespoons white vinegar
1 teaspoon salt

1) Mix the avocados and tomatoes together. Add the chili peppers, onion, vinegar, and salt. Mix well.

Makes 4 cups

Shrimp with Tangy Sauce

1 pound shrimp, cooked, shelled, and deveined
2 ounces butter
Juice of one lemon
3 tablespoons Worcestershire sauce
dash of salt
dash of pepper
2 drops Tabasco sauce

1) Mix all of the ingredients with the exception of the shrimp together.

2) Skewer the shrimp and place them on a bed of ice. Dip the shrimp into the sauce.

Serves 4

Artichoke Dip

¾ to 1 cup mayonnaise
½ cup grated mozzarella or pepper cheese
½ cup Parmesan cheese, grated
1 can chopped artichokes

1) Mix and put in baking dish. Bake at 350 degrees for 15 minutes. Serve with crackers.

Mrs. R. Ottonello
Sebastopol, CA

Bacon and Egg Rolls

8 eggs, beaten
¼ teaspoon salt
¼ teaspoon pepper
16 bacon strips, diced
1 cup ground beef
1 cup Cheddar cheese, grated
½ cup green pepper, chopped

1) Mix the eggs, salt and pepper together. Set aside.

2) Saute the bacon until it is crisp. Drain, reserving 2 tablespoons of bacon fat.

3) Saute the ground beef in the bacon fat until it begins to brown. Remove from heat and add the cheese and green pepper. Mix well. Add the bacon to the beef mixture. Mix well.

4) Place the 1/12 of the egg mixture in a well-oiled pan over a medium flame and cook for 1 minute. Turn over and place 2 tablespoons of the beef mixture onto the eggs and roll up.

Serves 12

Cheese Puffs

¼ cup water
⅛ cup butter
1 egg
3 ounces cream cheese
6 ounces American cheese spread

1) Mix the water and butter together and bring to a boil. Add the flour, stirring until a ball is formed. Remove and mix in the egg, beating until smooth and creamy. Stir in the cream cheese and American cheese.

2) Place the mixture, a teaspoon at a time, onto a well-oiled baking pan and bake at 400 degrees until browned.

Serves 4

Cheese Onion Bread

2 cups flour
2 teaspoons baking powder
½ tablespoon sugar
¼ teaspoon salt
¼ cup butter
1 cup Monterey Jack cheese
2 tablespoons onion, grated
1 teaspoons dried dill weed
¾ cup milk
1 egg, beaten

1) Mix the flour, baking powder, sugar, and salt together. Blend in the butter, until mixture becomes coarse, then add the Monterey Jack cheese, onions, and dill weed. Mix well.

2) Beat the milk and egg together and pour it into the cheese and flour mixture. Mix well.

3) Place in a lightly oiled loaf pan and bake at 350 degrees for 45 minutes.

Makes 1 loaf

Rumaki

chicken livers
bacon
water chestnuts
soy sauce
brown sugar

1) Soak livers in soy sauce for 24 hours. Cut into 1-inch pieces. Lightly brown bacon. Wrap a slice of water chestnut and a piece of liver in a piece of the bacon. Push a toothpick through the bacon, liver and water chestnut.

2) Roll in brown sugar, place on a cookie sheet and broil until bacon is crisp.

John D. Ashford
Phoenix, AZ

Curry Rumaki

¼ pound chicken livers, cut into
serving size pieces
4 bacon slices, cut in half crosswise
4 ounces water chestnuts, drained
¼ cup soy sauce
¼ teaspoon curry powder
¼ teaspoon ginger

1) Wrap each slice of bacon around a water chestnut and a piece of chicken liver. Fasten with a toothpick.

2) Mix curry powder, ginger, and soy sauce together. Add the rumaki and lightly toss. Refrigerate for 2 hours, tossing occasionally.

3) Place rumaki on broiler and cook for 12 minutes, turning often.

Serves 4

Wahini Tahini

1½ cups garbanzo beans, cooked and mashed
¾ cups tahini paste
1 garlic clove, mashed
juice of 2 lemons
½ teaspoon salt
½ teaspoon pepper
2 tablespoons hot water
1 teaspoon parsley, chopped

1) Mix the tahini paste, garbanzo beans, lemon juice, garlic, salt, and pepper together. Slowly add the hot water until the mixture is smooth and rich. Sprinkle with chopped parsley and serve with crackers or bread.

Serves 15

Stuffed Mushroom Marvel

1 cup white bread, cubed
24 extra large mushrooms
4 eggs
1 cup ricotta cheese
4 garlic cloves, minced
4 tablespoons parsley, chopped
dash of salt
dash of pepper
½ cup Parmesan cheese, grated

1) Place the bread cubes in water, squeeze dry, then shred. Add the eggs, ricotta, garlic, parsley, salt, and pepper. Mix well.

2) Stuff the mushrooms with the mixture and place on a lightly oiled baking dish, cap side down. Sprinkle with Parmesan and bake at 400 degrees for 15 to 20 minutes.

Serves 12

Kaye's Rye Bread Dip

1⅓ cups sour cream
1⅓ cups Hellman's Mayonnaise
2 teaspoons Beau Monde (spice)
2 teaspoons parsley flakes
2 teaspoons dill weed
2 teaspoons minced or chopped onion
2 packages Buddig corned beef, chopped
1 loaf light round rye bread

1) Mix all ingredients together in bowl. Cut center of bread out and place dip inside center. Cut up left over bread to dip.

Kaye A. Back
Summan, IN

Italian Red Peppers

4 red peppers, washed and drained
½ cup olive oil
1 ounce lemon juice
1 teaspoon salt
1 large garlic clove

1) Place peppers in an oven and bake at 450 degrees for 20 minutes or until the skin of the peppers begins to blacken. Turn often. Remove and let cool. Skin, slice, and remove seeds and ribs.

2) Mix the lemon juice, oil, garlic, and salt together. Add the red peppers, tossing to coat with the seasoning mixture. Refrigerate for at least 6 hours and serve.

Serves 6

Anchovy Canapes

4 ounces cream cheese
⅛ pound butter
½ ounce anchovy paste
4 slices pumpernickel bread, sliced thin
with crusts removed

1) Mix the anchovy paste, cheese, and butter together.

2) Cut the bread into small rectangles and make petite sandwiches with the anchovy mixture. Place the canapes on a baking pan and bake in a 400 degree oven until the bread is toasted.

Serves 8

Cream Cheese and Black Olive Dip

12 ounces softened cream cheese
4 teaspoons fresh lemon juice
2 teaspoons lemon rind, grated
5 cups black olives, pitted and chopped
16 ounces condensed black bean soup

1) Mix the cream cheese, lemon juice, and lemon rind together. Add the olives and the black bean soup. Mix well.

2) Chill before serving. Serve with tortilla chips.

Serves 12

Devilish Deviled Eggs

4 hard boiled eggs, sliced lengthwise
1 ounce butter, melted
1 ounce mayonnaise
¼ teaspoon thyme
¼ teaspoon salt
¼ teaspoon cayenne pepper
½ teaspoon lemon juice
¼ teaspoon powdered mustard
2 ounces bread crumbs, buttered and brown
¼ teaspoon paprika
1 ounce parsley, chopped

1) Mash the egg yolks in a bowl. Add the melted butter, mayonnaise, thyme, salt, cayenne pepper, lemon juice, and powdered mustard. Mix until rich and creamy.

2) Place mixture in the egg whites.

3) Mix the bread crumbs, paprika, and parsley together. Lightly dip the top portion of each egg into the mixture. Refrigerate for 45 minutes.

Serves 4

Cheese Square Puffs

1 loaf unsliced white bread (remove crust with serrated knife and cut in one inch or large squares)
1 cup (1 stick) butter
1 to 3 oz. cream cheese
¼ pound sharp cheese, cut into small pieces
2 egg whites

1) Beat two egg whites stiff, but not dry. Mix cream cheese and sharp cheese together. Thoroughly melt butter, then beat in egg whites and cheese mixture.

2) Hurriedly dunk bread cubes in mixture, about six at a time. Remove one at a time and gently scrape bottom of cubes with spoon. Put on wax paper or cookie sheet and freeze in air-tight bag until needed.

3) Bake at 400 degrees for about 10 minutes or until browned nicely. Can also be baked before freezing.

Mrs. Karl Thornton
Boise, ID

Pork Satay

¾ pound pork tenderloin, sliced
½ tablespoon garlic, pressed
½ tablespoon fresh ginger root, grated
½ teaspoon sugar
pinch of pepper
¼ cup soy sauce
⅛ cup water

1) Cut the pork into round pieces, roughly 1 inch in diameter. Flatten and place on a skewer.

2) Mix the remaining ingredients together. Marinate the pork in the mixture for 4 hours in the refrigerator.

3) Broil the skewers for 4 minutes on each side.

Serves 6

Deviled Crab

3 medium onions
3 medium bell peppers
1 16 ounce can tomatoes
2 6 ounce cans crab meat
1 cup bread crumbs
3 eggs
1 stick margarine or butter

1) Cut up onions and bell peppers. Melt margarine in saucepan. Add peppers and onions and cook until tender. Add tomatoes, bread crumbs, eggs and crab meat. Mix well.

2) Put in two 9-inch cake pans. Bake at 450 degrees until top is crusty (about 1 hour). Serve on crackers.

Bobby Bundy
Troy, AL

Tuna Twirls

1 can tuna
1 can peas/carrots
Bisquick
1 can mushroom soup

1) Prepare biscuit recipe for Bisquick. Roll out on board. Drain tuna and vegetables and combine. Save the juices.

2) Spread over dough and roll up. Cut and place like cinnamon rolls in 2 greased 7 x 10 x 2 inch pans. Dot with butter on top and bake at 375 degrees until biscuits are browned (10 to 20 minutes).

3) Combine the tuna and vegetable juices with the soup. Heat and serve with the biscuits. Cooked chicken may be substituted for the tuna.

Mrs. B. E. Haggstrom
Sandy, OR

SOUPS

Chicken Vegetable Soup

6 cups water
1 bay leaf
½ cup chopped carrots
1 (5 to 6 lbs.) cut up chicken
¼ cup chopped celery
½ cup chopped onion
2 cups cubed potatoes
1 teaspoon parsley
2 teaspoons salt
¼ teaspoon pepper

1) In a large kettle combine water, chicken pieces, onion, bay leaf, salt and pepper. Bring to boil and reduce heat. Simmer covered for about 1½ hours, or until chicken is tender.

2) Remove chicken and cut off bone when cooled. Cut in cubes. Discard bone and skin and bay leaf. Skim off fat.

3) Add vegetables to broth and boil until tender. Add cubed chicken and parsley and simmer about 8-10 minutes. Just before serving, if desired, add ½ teaspoon butter.

Serves 8

Margaret A. Morrison
Pittsburgh, PA

Light and Easy Minestrone Soup

20 ounces condensed beef bouillon
2½ cups water
½ cup macaroni
5 ounces frozen carrots
5 ounces frozen peas
5 ounces frozen Lima beans
1 large onion, chopped
dash of salt
dash of pepper
½ small cabbage, chopped
Parmesan cheese, grated

1) Bring the water and bouillon to a boil. Add the macaroni and cook for 5 to 7 minutes.

2) Add the vegetables, salt, and pepper, lower flame, and simmer until vegetables are soft. Top with Parmesan cheese.

Serves 4

Cheese and Onion Soup

½ cup Swiss cheese, grated
½ cup Provolone cheese, grated
2 onions, sliced
3 cups beef bouillon
¼ tablespoon butter
½ tablespoon flour
pinch of salt
pinch of pepper
4 hard slices French bread

1) Saute the onions in butter until brown. Gradually add in the flour, salt, pepper, and 2 tablespoons of bouillon. Mix well.

2) Pour onion mixture into the bouillon and bring to a boil. Lower flame and simmer for 15 minutes.

3) Toast the bread and then place at the bottom of bowls. Pour soup over bread, sprinkle cheese over top, and place bowls in broiler for 3 minutes, until a crust is formed.

Serves 4

New Orleans Gumbo

2 pound stewing chicken, cut into serving sized pieces
½ cup ham, diced
1 tablespoon butter
¼ cup onion, diced
pinch of thyme
⅛ cup parsley, chopped
4 cups boiling water
1 bay leaf
½ cup okra, sliced
¼ teaspoon salt
¼ teaspoon pepper
½ cup shrimp, shelled and deveined
½ quart stewing oysters, in liquid
1 cup cooked rice

1) Saute the chicken, ham, and butter in a large soup pot until the chicken browned. Add the onion, thyme, and parsley. Saute until the onion becomes transparent. Add the boiling water, bay leaf, okra, salt, and pepper and bring to a boil.

2) Lower flame and simmer and cook for 1 hour or until the chicken is tender.

3) Add the shrimp and the oysters and cook for an additional 10 minutes. Place ¼ cup cooked rice in a bowl and pour the gumbo on top.

Serves 4

Black Bean and Ham Soup

½ pound black beans, washed and drained
1 quart water
1 pound smoked ham hocks
½ cup celery, chopped
¾ cup onion, chopped
1 bay leaf
½ teaspoon salt
½ teaspoon pepper
2 tablespoons oil
¼ cup sherry
¼ cup green pepper, chopped
1 hard boiled egg, peeled and chopped
4 tablespoons sour cream

1) Place beans and water in a pot, bring to boiling and cook for 3 minutes. Remove, let cool, covered, for 1 hour.

2) Add the ham hocks, celery, onion, bay leaf, salt, pepper, and oil. Bring to boiling, lower flame, and simmer, covered for 2 hours. Remove ham hocks and bay leaf.

3) Puree the beans, place in pot. Remove the meat from the cooked ham hocks, discarding any fat and bones. Add meat and sherry to pot. Simmer over low flame until hot. Spoon into bowls, topping with green pepper, egg, and 1 tablespoon sour cream.

Serves 4

Cold Potato Soup

4 tablespoons butter
1 cup leeks, chopped
1⅓ cups water
1 teaspoon chicken stock base
20 ounces canned condensed cream of
potato soup, undiluted
1 cup milk
2 cups half and half

1) Saute the leeks in butter for 5 minutes. Add the water and chicken stock base. Heat to boiling, lower flame, cover, and simmer for 12 minutes. Stir in the potato soup, milk, and half and half. Chill.

2) Blend soup until rich and creamy and serve.

Serves 8

Cream of Mushroom Soup

2 pounds mushrooms
8 cups chicken broth
¼ cup butter
4 tablespoons flour
dash of salt
dash of pepper
1 cup heavy cream
½ cup dry sherry

1) Remove the mushroom stems, chop, and place the stems in a pan with the chicken broth. Bring to a boil, lower flame, and simmer for 25 minutes. Strain and set aside.

2) Slice the mushroom caps and saute in butter until brown. Add the flour, salt, and pepper. Stir in the chicken broth and bring to a boil. Lower flame and simmer for 5 minutes. Add the cream and sherry. Cook until hot.

Serves 8

Asparagus and Basil Soup

¼ cup butter
1 large yellow onion, chopped
2 large garlic cloves, chopped
¾ quarts chicken stock
1½ pounds asparagus
1 carrot, peeled and cut into bite sized pieces
4 fresh basil leaves
½ tablespoon dried tarragon
½ cup fresh parsley, stemmed and chopped
½ teaspoon salt
½ teaspoon pepper
dash of cayenne pepper

1) Saute the garlic and onions in garlic over a low flame for 20 minutes. Add the chicken stock and heat to boiling.

2) Cut the asparagus into fourths, reserving the tips. Place the pieces into the chicken stock. Add the carrots, basil, tarragon, parsley, salt, pepper, and cayenne. Simmer over a low flame, covered for 1 hour or until the vegetables are soft.

3) Remove the soup, let cool. Blend and strain until smooth.

4) Return the soup to the pan, add the asparagus tips, and simmer over a medium flame for 12 minutes or until the tips soften.

Serves 4

Quick Veggie-Beef Soup

1 pound stew meat, browned
1 pound ground beef, browned
1 cup cabbage, chopped
1 cup spinach, chopped
1 cup broccoli, chopped
1 cup carrots, sliced
3 medium potatoes, cubed
1 can (48 oz.) chicken broth
1 can (48 oz.) V-8 juice or tomato juice
mushrooms (or any veggie you like) to
fill the pot
salt and pepper to taste

1) Brown meats, do not drain. Add all other veggies, broth and juice.

2) Bring to a boil, reduce heat and simmer for one hour.

Serves 8

Mrs. R. L. Prater
Lincoln Park, MI

Orion's Onion Soup

5 large onions, sliced
½ cup butter
1 cup white wine
15 ounces consomme
10 ounces condensed beef bouillon
1 cup water
dash of salt
dash of pepper
⅛ cup brandy
Parmesan cheese, grated

1) Saute the onions in ¼ cup of butter until lightly browned. Place browned onions in a pot, and add wine, consomme, bouillon, and water.

2) Bring the soup to a boil, then lower flame and simmer for 25 to 30 minutes. Add salt and pepper while cooking.

3) Add brandy and cook for one minute before serving. Top with Parmesan cheese.

Serves 4

Chunky Cheese Soup

4 cups chicken consomme
4 slices of pumpernickel bread
1 tablespoon butter
4 eggs
2 cups Edam cheese, grated
4 slices Cheddar cheese
4 slices Provolone cheese

1) Heat consomme to boiling, lower flame, and simmer for 10 minutes.

2) Fry the pumpernickel in butter. Poach the eggs in the consomme, drain, and place over the fried bread in heated bowls. Pour the hot consomme over the eggs and bread, sprinkle with Edam cheese, and top with slices of Cheddar and Provolone.

Serves 4

Classic Vegetable and Chicken Soup

3 pound stewing chicken, cut into serving
sized pieces
8 cups water
¾ cups carrots, diced
¾ cup parsley, diced
¾ cup onion, diced
¾ cup cabbage, chopped
⅓ cup celery, chopped
⅓ cup canned tomatoes, drained
½ tablespoon salt
¼ teaspoon black pepper

1) Place the chicken in water and bring to a boil.
Add the vegetables, salt, and pepper, and bring to
a boil. Lower the flame, cover, and simmer for 2½
hours or until the chicken is tender.

2) Remove the chicken from the soup and remove
the meat from the bones. Discard the bones, return
the meat to soup and serve.

Serves 4

New England's Finest Clam Chowder

3 slices bacon, chopped
2 cups onion, chopped
3 cups potatoes, peeled and cubed
1½ cups water
1 teaspoon salt
½ teaspoon pepper
1½ pints fresh clams, shucked
3 cups half and half
2 tablespoons butter

1) Saute the bacon until almost crispy. Add the onions and continue to cook until onions become transparent. Add the potatoes, water, salt, and pepper. Cook medium flame, uncovered for 12 to 15 minutes or until the potatoes are soft.

2) Drain and chop the clams, reserving the liquid. Add the clams, ¾ cup clam liquid, butter, and half and half to the potato mixture. Mix well. Cook for 3 to 5 minutes over a medium flame.

Serves 6

Beet Borscht

6 beets
2 pounds beef brisket, cut into bite sized chunks
2 onions, sliced
2 celery stalks, cut into bite sized chunks
4 carrots, sliced
2 bay leaves
dash of salt
6 ounces canned tomato paste
2 teaspoons sugar
1 cabbage, shredded

1) Place 4 sliced beets, brisket, onion, celery, carrots, bay leaves, and salt in a pot and simmer over a low flame for 2½ hours.

2) Shred the remaining 2 beets and add to the heated mixture. Stir in the tomato paste and sugar. Simmer, covered for 25 minutes. Remove the bay leaves and chill.

3) Skim the fat from the surface of the soup. Heat over a medium flame until boiling, add the cabbage and cook for 15 minutes until the cabbage is soft.

Serves 8

Grandma's Splendorous Split Pea Soup

1 cup dried yellow split peas, rinsed
water
1 small ham bone
1 small onion
1 small carrot, quartered
1 celery rib, chopped
pinch of salt
pinch of pepper
1 small potato, diced

1) Place peas in enough water to cover and allow to soak overnight.

2) Drain the peas and place in a pot with enough water to cover. Add the ham bone, onion, carrot, celery, salt, and pepper. Bring to a boil, cover, and simmer for 1½ to 2 hours or until peas are soft. Add the potato and cook for an additional ½ hour.

3) Blend soup so that it is smooth and creamy before serving. Add water if necessary.

Serves 4

Broccoli Soup with Leeks

2 small leeks, trimmed
½ teaspoon cider vinegar
water
⅓ cup butter, melted
1 small onion, chopped
1 teaspoon salt
1 teaspoon pepper
1 potato, peeled and sliced
1 quart chicken broth
1 broccoli bunch, trimmed
1 watercress bunch, rinsed, stemmed, and dried
¼ cup heavy cream

1) Slice the leeks in half lengthwise and soak in the vinegar and enough water to cover for 20. Remove the leeks, rinse, dry, and chop.

2) Place the leeks, onions, salt and pepper in melted butter, and saute for 10 to 15 minutes or until the vegetables are very soft. Add the potatoes and broth and simmer uncovered for an additional 15 minutes.

3) Slice the broccoli stalks. Place the florets and sliced stalks in the soup and simmer for 12 minutes. Remove from the stove, add the watercress, and let stand for 3 minutes.

4) Blend the soup until smooth, gradually add the cream, and simmer until warm.

Serves 4

Cabbage Soup

3 pounds chopped beef
1 cup chopped celery
2 cans kidney beans
salt and pepper to taste
1 large onion, chopped
2 cans tomatoes
1 small hard cabbage, quartered

1) Boil chopped beef until tender. Add onions and celery. Boil 10 minutes. Cool 1 hour.

2) Add tomatoes and kidney beans. Cook 30 minutes more. Add cabbage, cook until cabbage is tender, about 20 minutes.

Serves 8

Mrs. Ronald K. Bailey
St. Louis, MO

Mexican Meatball Soup

1 large carrot, chopped
1 small onion, chopped
⅛ cup olive oil
1½ cups chicken stock
1½ cups water
15 ounces consomme
⅛ cup tomato sauce
½ pound lean ground beef
2 tablespoons rice
1 tablespoon chopped parsley
1 egg
½ teaspoons salt
¼ teaspoon pepper
5 ounces frozen peas
1 tablespoon fresh cilantro, chopped

1) Saute the carrots and onion in the olive oil. Add the chicken stock, water, consomme, and tomato sauce. Simmer over low flame for 12 to 15 minutes.

2) Mix the beef, rice, egg, parsley, salt and pepper together to form small meat balls.

3) Bring the soup to a boil, add the meat balls, lower flame and simmer for 20 to 25 minutes. Add the peas and cilantro and cook for an additional 5 minutes.

Serves 4

Swiss Cheese and Vegetable Soup

2 cups Swiss cheese, grated
2 heads of cabbage, shredded
2 large potatoes, sliced
2 quarts whole milk
4 tablespoons butter
¼ teaspoon salt
¼ teaspoon pepper

1) Place potatoes and cabbage in boiling water and cook until soft. Drain and blend together with a fork.

2) Add butter, milk, salt, and pepper. Simmer over a low flame for 15 minutes. Remove and spoon into bowls. Sprinkle with Swiss cheese. Place under a broiler for 3 minutes or until crust forms.

Serves 4

Simple Chicken Soup

3 pounds chicken wings, necks, and backs
2 small carrots, peeled
3 celery stalks, cut into large pieces
⅓ cup onions, chopped
½ teaspoon salt
½ teaspoon pepper
¾ tablespoon parsley, chopped
water

1) Place all of the ingredients into a large soup pot, with enough water to cover. Cover and bring to a boil. Skim off the scum, re-cover, lower heat, and simmer for 1¾ hours.

Serves 4

Beef Onion Soup

¼ cup butter
4 onions, sliced thinly
1½ tablespoons flour
5 cups beef stock
¼ teaspoon pepper
¼ cup sherry
4 slices toasted French bread, sliced 1 inch thick
4 slices Swiss cheese
¼ cup Parmesan cheese, grated

1) Saute the onions in the butter until they become golden. Add the flour and cook, stirring often, until the flour begins to brown. Slowly add the beef stock and pepper. Simmer over a low flame, covered, for 30 minutes. Stir often. Add the sherry.

2) Place a slice of bread and cheese in a bowl, pour the hot soup over the top, sprinkle with Parmesan cheese, and broil until the cheese melts.

Serves 4

Quick and Easy Gazpacho Soup

10 ounces canned condensed tomato bisque soup
10 ounces water, boiling
1 beef bouillon cube
1 tomato, chopped
2 tablespoons red wine vinegar
½ tablespoon oil
½ teaspoon Worcestershire
3 squirts Tabasco sauce
1 tablespoon onion, minced
2 tablespoons green pepper, chopped
½ teaspoon salt

1) Dissolve the bouillon cube in the boiling water. Slowly add to the soup. Mix well.

2) Stir in the remaining ingredients, cover, and chill.

Serves 4

Tomato Soup with Clam Broth

2 cups clam broth
2 cups tomato juice
4 dashes Tabasco sauce
Juice of a lemon
½ teaspoon pepper
6 tablespoons plain yogurt
3 teaspoons chives, chopped

1) Pour the clam broth and tomato juice into a pan and simmer until hot. Add the Tabasco sauce, lemon juice, and pepper.

2) Spoon the soup into bowls and top with yogurt and chives.

Serves 6

Chicken Marsala Soup

1 whole chicken breast, poached, skinned, boned, and cut thinly
4 cups chicken stock
3 tablespoons pine nuts, chopped
⅓ cup Marsala
¾ teaspoon saffron threads
2 egg yolks
⅓ cup heavy cream

1) Place the chicken, stock and pine nuts in a pan and heat to boiling. Lower flame and simmer for 5 minutes. Add the Marsala and the saffron and simmer for an additional 3 minutes. Remove and let stand.

2) Blend the egg yolks and heavy cream together. Gradually pour the cream mixture into the hot soup, stirring briskly.

Serves 4

SALADS

Poly's Shrimp Salad

Salad:
½ pounds boiled shrimp, cold (boil in water
with ½ lemon squeezed, and 1 clove
garlic, smashed)
½ green pepper, chopped
2 tomatoes, chopped
1 avocado, peeled and chopped
3 stalks, peeled and chopped
½ head lettuce, torn into pieces
1 cucumber, chopped (skin optional)

Dressing:
½ lemon, squeezed
¼ cup mayonnaise
1 tablespoon sour cream
1 clove garlic, chopped fine
salt and pepper to taste

1) Combine all ingredients in large salad bowl.
Toss well.

2) Mix dressing thoroughly, pour over salad. Toss
lightly. Chill for 30 minutes.

Serves 8

Mrs. Louis J. Pekar
Port LaVaca, TX

Spinach Salad

2 red onions, sliced thinly
1 pound fresh spinach, washed, dried
and stemmed
1 cup walnuts, chopped and toasted
1 cup raisins, washed, drained, and dried

1) Place the onion in a large bowl. Add the spinach on top. Sprinkle with raisins and nuts. Serve with your favorite French dressing.

Serves 8

Pear and Roquefort Salad

4 ounces Roquefort cheese
8 pears, peeled, split, and cored
8 tablespoons cream cheese
1 cup cream
1 ounce butter
dash of paprika
dash of salt

1) Mix the butter an Roquefort together until smooth. Place the mixture into the pears. Blend the cream and the cream cheese until the mixture will pour.

2) Place the pears on the lettuce and pour the cream cheese mixture over them. Sprinkle with paprika. Chill before serving.

Serves 8

Chicken and Egg Salad

4 cups cooked chicken (white meat), sliced
into thin strips
4 hard boiled eggs, chopped
2 tablespoons onion, chopped
2 cups celery, diced
½ cup mayonnaise
½ teaspoon salt
½ teaspoon pepper
8 whole tomatoes
2 heads lettuce, shredded

1) Combine all of the ingredients with the exception of the tomatoes and lettuce. Toss lightly.

2) Place the shredded lettuce on a serving dish. Slice the tops off of the tomatoes and remove pulp. Fill the tomatoes with chicken salad and arrange on the shredded lettuce. Chill and serve.

Serves 8

Green Salad with Tangy Oil and Vinegar Dressing

2 heads Boston lettuce
2 heads butter lettuce
1 head romaine lettuce
2 Belgian endives
1 garlic clove
10 tablespoons olive oil
6 tablespoons herb vinegar
1 teaspoon salt
1 teaspoon pepper

1) Wash and separate the lettuce. Drain. Refrigerate until crisp. Rub the inside of a cold salad bowl with garlic. Tear the lettuce and place into the bowl.

2) Combine the olive oil, herb vinegar, salt, and pepper. Mix well. Pour over the salad and serve.

Serves 10

Independence Day Cole Slaw

1 cup vinegar
½ teaspoon celery seeds
½ teaspoon dry mustard
½ cups sugar
1 small head cabbage, shredded
½ onion, chopped
½ green pepper, cored, seeded, and shredded
ice water

1) Mix the vinegar, celery seeds, mustard, and sugar in a pan and bring to a boil. Stir until the sugar dissolves. Continue to boil for 15 minutes. Let cool.

2) Combine the cabbage, onion, and green pepper, and place in enough ice water to cover for 1 hour. Drain thoroughly. Combine vegetables with dressing an refrigerate overnight.

Serves 6

Egg Salad

6 hard boiled eggs, peeled and chopped
3 scallions, sliced
3 celery ribs, chopped
1 tablespoon caraway seeds
6 ounces bacon, cut into bite-sized pieces,
cooked until crisp, and drained
2 tablespoons white horseradish
½ cup mayonnaise
¼ cup fresh parsley, chopped

1) Combine the eggs, scallions, celery, caraway seeds, and bacon. Toss lightly. Combine the mayonnaise and horseradish and fold the mixture into the salad. Sprinkle with parsley and serve.

Serves 4

Mixed Seafood Mold

1 cup mayonnaise
1 (8 ounces) can or package cooked crabmeat
1 pound frozen shrimp
2 full size onions, chopped
2 stalks celery, chopped
1 can tomato soup
1 (8 ounces) package cream cheese
2 packages gelatin

1) Add the cream cheese to the tomato soup. Blend while heating and let cool. In small bowl, dissolve the gelatin in ¼ cup cold water. Mix with soup mixture until dissolved.

2) In separate bowl, add the mayonnaise to the seafood, celery, onion and a dash each of Worcestershire Sauce and Tabasco. Mix together with soup and pour into mold. Refrigerate until mold sets. Best if chilled overnight.

Serves 6

Mrs. Sandra Snyder
Chatsworth, CA

Cucumber and Grape Salad

Salad:
1 head romaine lettuce
1 cucumber, peeled and sliced thinly
¾ cup seedless grapes
2 tablespoons fresh dill, chopped

Dressing:
¾ cup olive oil
¼ cup lemon juice
½ teaspoon sugar
½ teaspoon salt
½ teaspoon pepper

1) Combine and mix the ingredients for the dressing. Place in refrigerator.

2) Combine and mix the ingredients for the salad. Add dressing and toss.

Serves 4

Chef Salad Supreme

2 head lettuce, washed, torn, drained, dried
2 head endive, curled
2 large scoops cottage cheese
2 cups shredded cooked turkey
2 cups shredded cooked ham
1 cup Roquefort cheese, crumbled
8 hard boiled eggs, sliced
½ cup scallions, chopped
1 cup carrots, chopped
½ cup raisins
1 cup mushrooms, sliced
1 cup Cheddar, shredded
1 cup Provolone, shredded

1) Toss the lettuce together. Place the cottage cheese in the center of the lettuce. Arrange the shredded meats around the salad.

2) Sprinkle the Roquefort cheese on top. Add the eggs, scallions, carrots, raisins, and mushrooms. Top with the Cheddar and Provolone cheese.

Serves 10

Citrus Chicken Salad

2 cups cooked chicken (white meat), diced
1½ cups grapefruit sections
2 cups celery, diced
¼ teaspoon lime peel, grated
1½ tablespoons lime juice
¼ cup mayonnaise
¼ teaspoon salt
¼ teaspoon pepper
2 small oranges, peeled and sliced
2 heads endive, snipped

1) Combine the chicken, grapefruit, and celery.

2) Add the salt, pepper, lime juice and peel to the mayonnaise. Beat until light and airy. Fold the mayonnaise mixture into the chicken.

3) Arrange a salad bowl with the endive. Place the chicken salad in the center, arranging the orange slices around the edge. Chill and serve.

Serves 4

Simple Chef's Salad

1 head lettuce
1 tomato, cut into wedges
1 tablespoon chives, diced
¼ pound cooked chicken (white meat), sliced
¼ pound cup cooked ham, sliced
¼ pound Swiss cheese, sliced

1) Combine the lettuce, tomatoes, chives, chicken, ham, and cheese. Serve with your favorite herb dressing.

Serves 4

Caesar Salad

⅓ cup olive oil
1 garlic clove, crushed
½ cup bread cubes, stale
2 small heads romaine lettuce, washed and dried
pinch of salt
pinch of pepper
1 egg, boiled for one minute
1 lemon, halved
½ tablespoon Worcestershire sauce
4 anchovy fillets, chopped
¼ cup Parmesan cheese, grated

1) Combine the oil and the garlic and allow to stand overnight. Remove garlic.

2) Brown the bread crumbs in 2 tablespoons of the oil. Drain and set aside.

3) Place the lettuce in a large bowl, and add salt, pepper, and the remaining oil. Break open the egg over the salad and toss. Squeeze the lemon over the salad. Add the anchovies, Worcestershire sauce, and Parmesan. Toss. Add the bread cubes and toss again.

Serves 4

Red Potato and Egg Salad

6 red potatoes, boiled and cut in half
3 hard boiled eggs, peeled and halved
1 scallion, sliced
1 small carrot, peeled and grated
1 tablespoon fresh parsley, chopped
1 tablespoon caraway seeds
1½ tablespoons fresh dill, chopped
¼ teaspoon salt
¼ teaspoon freshly ground black pepper
⅓ cup sour cream
⅓ cup mayonnaise

1) Combine the potatoes, eggs, scallions, and carrots. Add the parsley, caraway, dill, salt, and pepper. Toss lightly.

2) Combine the mayonnaise and sour cream and fold into the potato egg mixture. Refrigerate for 3 hours and serve.

Serves 4

Shrimp and Macaroni Salad

1 pound cleaned and boiled shrimp, chopped
1 pound cooked macaroni shells
6 boiled eggs, chopped
1 medium onion, finely chopped
1 bell pepper, finely chopped
1 dill pickle, finely chopped (substitute sweet if preferred)
¼ cup finely chopped olives (with pimento)
1 cup mayonnaise
¼ cup mayonnaise
¼ cup mustard
salt and pepper to taste

1) Mix all ingredients and store in a covered bowl in the refrigerator until ready to serve.

2) The flavors will blend better if the salad is made one day, stored in the refrigerator overnight and then served the next day. If the salad is stored overnight, the macaroni may soak up your mayonnaise and dry out your salad. If this happens simply add a small amount of mayonnaise to moisten your salad.

Serves 8

Barbara Alday
Panacea, FL

Mushroom Salad with Madeira Wine

½ pound fresh mushrooms, rinsed and sliced
juice of 1 lemon
½ tablespoon Madeira wine
⅓ cup mayonnaise
1½ teaspoons tomato paste
1 teaspoon fresh tarragon, chopped

1) Combine all of the ingredients with the exception of the mushrooms and the lemon juice. Sprinkle the mushrooms with lemon juice. Add to other ingredients, stir, cover, and chill.

Serves 4

Cheese, Honey and Grape Salad

½ cup cream
1 cup sour cream
2 tablespoons honey
2 cups Cheddar cheese, cubed
1 cup cream cheese
4 cups seedless grapes

1) Place enough cream in the sour cream to thin. Add 2 tablespoons of honey. Mix.

2) Combine the cheeses, add grapes, and toss. Chill and serve.

Serves 6

California Chicken Salad

6 cups cooked chicken (white meat)
2 avocados, diced
¾ cup green pepper diced
2 cups celery, diced
½ cup scallions, diced
2 cups mayonnaise
½ teaspoon cayenne pepper
½ teaspoon salt
½ teaspoon pepper
Juice of a lemon
1 cup sour cream
pinch of paprika

1) Combine the chicken, avocados, green pepper, celery, and scallions together. Mix the sour cream, mayonnaise, lemon juice, cayenne, salt, and pepper together.

2) Pour the tangy dressing over the chicken. Lightly toss and sprinkle with paprika.

Serves 8

Mediterranean Salad

¾ pound fresh green beans, washed and trimmed
1 large tomato, cut into wedges
1 small onion, sliced
⅓ cup olives, pitted
1 ounce anchovy fillets
2 hard boiled eggs, sliced
10 ounces canned tuna, drained and chunked

1) Place the green beans in boiling water and cook, covered for 15 minutes or until they begin to soften. Drain and place in cold water. Drain again. Pour ⅓ cup of your favorite oil and vinegar dressing and toss well. Refrigerate the beans for 1 hour.

2) Place the marinated beans in a salad bowl. Add the tomatoes, onions, olives and anchovy fillets. Toss lightly. Add the egg and tuna. Toss lightly. Serve with remaining oil and vinegar dressing.

Serves 4

Tomato and Basil Salad

3 large whole tomatoes, peeled and sliced
1 tablespoon fresh basil leaves, chopped
2 tablespoons scallions, chopped
⅓ cup olive oil
2 tablespoons vinegar
¾ teaspoon Worcestershire sauce
½ garlic clove, chopped
¼ teaspoon sugar
½ teaspoon salt
½ teaspoon pepper

1) Arrange the tomato slices in a serving bowl. Sprinkle with basil and scallions.

2) Combine the oil, vinegar, Worcestershire, garlic, and sugar, salt and pepper. Mix well, pour over the tomatoes and chill.

Serves 4

Penny Carrot Salad

Salad:
3 pounds carrots, sliced
water
1 onion, diced
1 green pepper

Dressing:
1 can tomato soup
½ cup salad oil
½ cup vinegar
1 teaspoon Worcestershire
1 teaspoon yellow mustard
1 teaspoon salt

1) Cook 3 lbs. sliced carrots until tender. Do not overcook carrots. Drain and cool in ice water. Add 1 finely diced onion, 1 diced green pepper.

2) For dressing, mix 1 can tomato soup, ½ cup salad oil, ½ cup vinegar, 1 teaspoon Worcestershire Sauce, 1 teaspoon yellow mustard, ½ teaspoon salt Blend and beat well the dressing ingredients. Pour over carrots, onions, pepper. Mix and marinate for 1 day. Keeps well in refrigerator.

Serves 6

Mrs. Gerhard Janz
Wisconsin Rapids, WI

Swiss Cheese and Carrot Salad

1 pound Swiss cheese, sliced thinly
2 heads butter lettuce, washed, torn, and chilled
2 heads lettuce, washed, torn, and chilled
2 heads endive, washed, curled, and chilled
1 cup carrots, shredded

1) Marinate the Swiss cheese in your favorite French dressing for 1 hour. Drain.

2) Toss the lettuce and the carrots together. Arrange the marinated cheese on top. Chill and serve.

Serves 8

Green Pea Salad

Salad:
1 box frozen green peas (do not thaw)
½ cup diced water chestnuts
½ cup diced celery
½ cup sliced green onions
½ cup diced sweet pickles
¼ cup diced red pepper
3 slices crisp fried bacon reserve
2 hard boiled eggs, diced

Dressing:
½ cup mayonnaise
1 teaspoon fresh dill, chopped (or
½ teaspoon dried)
2 teaspoons dill pickle juice
salt and pepper

1) Mix together salad ingredients and dressing ingredients separately. Add dressing to salad. Toss well. Chill several hours. When ready to serve crumble bacon over top.

Serves 6

Mrs. Taft Mitchell
Ventura, CA

Chicken Salad with Walnuts

2 cups cooked chicken (white meat), diced
2 cups walnut meats, coarsely chopped
1½ cups celery, chopped
¼ cup onion, chopped
¾ cup mayonnaise
2 hard boiled eggs, chopped
2 tablespoons juice from lemon
⅓ cup sour cream

1) Mix the chicken, walnuts, celery, onions, mayonnaise, and eggs together.

2) Combine the lemon juice and sour cream, fold into the chicken and walnut mixture. Chill and serve.

Serves 4

Holiday Fruit Salad

1 pound red seeded grapes
1 large can pineapple tidbits, drained
¼ lb. shelled pecans
1 package large marshmallows, quartered

Dressing:
4 egg yolks
¼ teaspoon mustard
pinch of salt
juice of one lemon
1 pint heavy cream, whipped

1) Whip the cream until it forms soft, firm peaks. Refrigerate. stir remaining ingredients for dressing together and boil over low flame until sauce thickens. Remove from heat and cool thoroughly.

2) When cool add the whipped cream. Add dressing to salad and mix well. Place in refrigerator overnight. Garnish with mint and maraschino cherries before serving.

Serves 4

Myrtle Sexton
Erick, OK

DESSERTS

Pound Cake

2 sticks butter
1 (8 oz.) package cream cheese
2 cups sugar
5 large eggs
3 cups all-purpose flour
½ teaspoon salt
2 teaspoons baking powder
1 teaspoon vanilla extract
1 teaspoon lemon extract

1) Sift together flour, salt, and baking powder. Set aside.

2) Blend butter, cream cheese, sugar, eggs, vanilla and lemon. Gradually combine the flour mixture with the moist ingredients.

3) Pour batter into a well greased loaf pan. Bake at 350 degrees for 1 to 1¼ hours.

Serves 6

Annie G. Wade
Thomasville, GA

Black Pepper and Pecan Brownies

4½ ounces unsweetened chocolate
6 ounces sweet butter
⅛ teaspoon salt
1 teaspoon powdered instant coffee
1¼ teaspoon ground black pepper
1½ teaspoon vanilla extract
1¼ cups brown sugar
3 eggs
¾ cup sifted sugar
4½ ounces pecans

1) Preheat oven to 375 degrees. Butter a 9" square pan.

2) Melt the chocolate. Let cool until warm.

3) Cream the butter and beat in the salt, coffee, pepper, vanilla, and sugar until mixture is well blended. Add the eggs one by one, beating lightly. Add in the chocolate and the flour, beating lightly. Stir in the pecans.

4) Pour the mixture into the pan, smooth the top, and bake for 25 to 30 minutes until brownies are moist. Let cool for 20 minutes. Refrigerate until firm.

Makes 24 brownies

Apricot Cake

2 cups sifted flour
1 teaspoon baking soda
1 teaspoon baking powder
⅛ teaspoon salt
1 teaspoon cinnamon
3 eggs
¼ cup milk
1 teaspoon allspice
¾ cup shortening
1 cup sugar
1 can Solo apricots
½ cup chopped walnuts
8 oz. heavy cream

1) Sift together flour, soda, baking powder, salt and spices. Cream shortening with sugar, add milk and apricots. Mix in eggs, gradually combine dry ingredients. Fold in nuts.

2) Pour into greased 9 x 13 inch pan. Bake at 350 degrees for 25 to 30 minutes. Top with whipped cream.

Serves 6

Mrs. Louise Godbey
Omaha, NE

Lemon Chocolate Truffles

7 ounces bittersweet chocolate
½ cup whipping cream
½ cup powdered sugar, sifted
2 tablespoons butter
2 egg yolks
1 teaspoon fresh lemon juice
5 tablespoons unsweetened cocoa powder
Coating (see below)

1) Melt the chocolate, whipping cream and butter together. Mix until smooth. Let cool.

2) Stir egg yolk, sugar and lemon juice into cooled mixture.

3) Refrigerate for 4 hours.

4) With buttered hands, roll a small handful of the refrigerated mixture into a ball and through the cocoa powder, dusting the truffle thoroughly.

5) Place dusted truffles in refrigerator for 1 hour.

Coating

3½ ounces bittersweet chocolate

1) Melt chocolate. Let cool.

2) Dip dusted and refrigerated truffles into cooled melted chocolate and place on wax paper. Spoon excess chocolate coating on top of truffles.

3) Refrigerate for 2 hours.

Makes 2-3 dozen truffles

Pumpkin Bread

3 cups sugar
1 teaspoon cinnamon
2 cups pumpkin
1 cup nuts
1 cup Mazola oil
1 teaspoon nutmeg
3½ cups flour
4 eggs
⅔ cup water
2 teaspoons baking soda
1½ teaspoons salt

1) Stir together dry ingredients and set aside.

2) Combine moist ingredients, blending well. Gradually add dry ingredients. Mix thoroughly.

3) Pour into 3 loaf pans. Bake at 350 degrees for 1 hour.

Serves 6

Maxine Patterson
Rapid City, SD

Pumpkin Cookies

1 egg
½ cup Crisco shortening
1 cup pumpkin
2 cups flour
1 teaspoon soda
1 teaspoon baking powder
1 teaspoon cinnamon
½ teaspoon salt
1 cup raisins
½ cup nuts

1) Combine dry ingredients and set aside.

2) Beat together moist ingredients until creamy, gradually adding flour mixture. Drop by teaspoonfuls on greased baking sheet and mash down with fork.

3) Bake at 400 degrees for 12 to 15 minutes. Double recipe for more cookies.

Serves 4

Mrs. Mary J. Reedy
Wellington, KS

Hawaiian Chocolate Brownies

2½ cups sugar
1½ cups butter
5 ounces bitter dark chocolate
2 cups flour, sifted
6 eggs
1 cup macadamia nuts, almonds or hazelnuts
Fudge (see below)

1) Preheat oven to 350 degrees. Line a baking pan (approx. 15″ x 15″) with parchment paper.

2) Melt the sugar, butter and chocolate together.

3) Blend in flour, eggs and nuts.

4) Bake for 30 minutes. Let cool.

Fudge

1 cup heavy cream
12 ounces dark chocolate

1) Heat up the cream. Stir in the chocolate until the mixture is smooth. Frost the cooled brownies.

Serves 10

Soft Sugar Cookies

½ cup shortening
1 cup sugar
1 egg
3¼ cups flour
½ teaspoon baking soda
1 teaspoon baking powder
½ teaspoon salt
¼ teaspoon nutmeg
½ cup sour cream

1) Cream shortening and sugar. Add egg. Sift dry ingredients and add alternately with sour cream. Chill dough 1 hour.

2) Roll out on floured board. Cut with glass or cookie cutter. Place on lightly greased cookie sheet. Bake at 350 degrees for 10 minutes, until lightly browned.

Serves 6

R. J. Griesinger
Adrian, MI

Fudgiest Fudge Cake

½ cup butter
1½ cups sugar
2 egg yolks
½ cup sugar
4 ounces melted chocolate
½ cup warm water
½ buttermilk
2½ cups flour, sifted with 1 teaspoon soda
2 egg whites
½ teaspoon cinnamon
¼ teaspoon ground cloves
½ cups chopped raisins
Frosting (see pg. 99)

1) Cream butter and beat in 1½ cups of sugar. Beat egg yolks with ½ cups of sugar until light. Combine two mixtures.

2) Alternately mix in melted chocolate, warm water, buttemilk and flour.

3) Beat in egg whites.

4) Pour mixture into baking pan.

5) Place spices and raisins on top.

6) Bake for 20 minutes. Remove and let cool.

Frosting

2 cups granulated sugar
⅔ cups milk
2 squares chocolate
2 tablespoons light corn syrup
2 tablespoons butter
1 teaspoon vanilla

1) Shave chocolate into saucepan.

2) Stir in sugar, milk and corn syrup until sugar is dissolved. Cook on medium heat until a teaspoon of syrup forms a soft ball when dropped in a glass of cold water.

3) Remove from heat and mix in butter. Let cool until lukewarm.

4) Beat in vanilla until frosting is thick.

5) Frost top and sides of cake.

Serves 10

Oatmeal Butterscotch Cookies

1 cup brown sugar
1 egg
1 cup Steel Cut oatmeal
1 cup flaked coconut
½ teaspoon salt
1 (6 oz.) package butterscotch chips
½ cup butter
½ teaspoon vanilla
1 cup flour
½ teaspoon baking powder
½ teaspoon baking soda

1) Cream sugar, butter and vanilla. Add egg, flour and baking soda, mix well. Add oats, coconut and chips.

2) Drop on greased cookie sheet. Bake 8 to 10 minutes at 350 degrees.

Serves 6

Julia D. Sikes
Fredericktown, MO

Irish Potato Cake

2 cups sugar
⅔ cup butter
1 cup warm mashed potatoes
1 ounce unsweetened chocolate
2 cups flour
2 teaspoons baking powder
½ teaspoon salt
½ cup buttermilk
1 cup chopped walnuts
1 teaspoon cloves
1 teaspoon cinnamon
1 teaspoon nutmeg
1 teaspoon vanilla
4 eggs separated

1) Mix together sugar and butter. Stir in chocolate and mashed potatoes.

2) Mix in flour, baking powder, salt. Stir in buttermilk, walnuts, spices and vanilla.

3) Beat egg whites and fold into mixture.

4) Pour mixture into baking pan and bake at 350 degrees for 35-40 minutes. Let cool.

Serves 8-10

Applesauce and Oatmeal Bars

1¼ cups flour
1 cup brown sugar
¾ cups shortening
1¼ cups quick oatmeal
1 cup applesauce with pinch of nutmeg
and cinnamon

1) Mix flour, sugar and shortening together. Add oats.

2) In 8 x 8 inch pan, put half the mixture and pat down with hands, pour applesauce over top of mixture, staying about ½ inch from sides. Cover with remaining oat mixture and pat firmly. Bake at 350 degrees for 40 minutes.

Serves 4

Lois Nerby
Almay, WI

Persimmon Pudding

1 cup flour
½ teaspoon salt
½ teaspoon baking soda
¾ cup sugar
1 cup persimmon pulp
2 eggs, beaten
1 cup milk
½ teaspoon grated lemon rind
2 teaspoons butter

1) Pre-heat oven to 350 degrees.

2) Sift together flour, salt, baking soda and sugar. Add persimmon pulp to the flour mixture along with remaining ingredients. Mix well, turn into a well greased, lightly floured baking dish (8 x 8 x 2 inch). Bake for 50 minutes. Serve with hard sauce or lemon sauce or whipped cream.

Serves 6

Mabel L. Hockstock
Venice, CA

Pina Colada Bread Pudding

6 slices white or whole wheat bread
2 cups milk
½ cup raisins
½ cup coconut, shredded or flaked
1 (8 oz.) can crushed pineapple with juice
½ stick margarine, melted
¾ cup sugar
2 eggs, well beaten
1 teaspoon vanilla (or 1 teaspoon rum extract)

1) Break bread into small pieces, add to milk in bowl and soak. Use hands to crush bread. Squeeze well. Add all other ingredients and mix well.

2) Grease casserole with margarine or butter, pour in pudding. Bake at 350 degrees for 45 minutes (or until very firm). Serve with whipped cream topping, if desired.

Serves 8

Olene Brown
Henryetta, OK

Chocolate Raspberry Macadamia Nut Cake

1 cup granulated sugar
¼ cup water
1 tablespoon coffee powder
6 ounces semisweet chocolate, broken
1 teaspoon almond extract
½ cup unsalted butter
8 eggs, separate yolks and white
1 cup macadamia nuts
2 cups raspberries
Frosting (see pg. 106)

1) Preheat oven to 350 degrees. Butter and flour two 9 inch cake pans.

2) Melt the sugar, water, and coffee powder together, over medium to high heat, stirring constantly for 4 minutes.

3) Remove from heat. Stir in the chocolate and almond extract. Continue to stir until all of the chocolate has melted, and the mixture is smooth. Let cool.

4) Beat butter until light and fluffy. Add in the egg yolks, one by one, and continue to beat. Stir in the cooled chocolate mixture. Stir in the macadamia nuts.

5) Beat egg whites until stiff. Fold one quarter of the egg whites into the chocolate mixture. Carefully fold in the remaining three quarters of the egg whites. Pour equal halves of the batter into the buttered and floured 9 inch cake pans.

6) Bake for 25-30 minutes or until the cake separates from the edge of the pan. Let cool.

Frosting

6 ounces semisweet chocolate, broken
¼ cup water
1 tablespoon coffee powder
1 cup unsalted butter
3 egg yolks
1 cup sifted powdered sugar
¼ cup macadamia nuts, ground

1) Mix chocolate, water and coffee powder over low heat until smooth. Let cool.

2) Cream the butter until fluffy. Beat in egg yolks, one by one. Beat in the cooled chocolate mixture. Beat in the powdered sugar. Refrigerate until thick.

3) Frost the top of one cake layer. Mash 1 cup raspberries and spread across frosting. Place other cake layer on top of first and frost the top and sides of the cake. Press ground macadamia nuts around side of cake. Arrange remaining cup of raspberries on top of cake.

Serves 10-12

Christmas Pudding

1 cup dates, chopped
½ cup currants
milk
dried fruit mixture
2 packages Knox gelatin
1 cup water
4 tablespoons cocoa
2 cups sugar
4 egg yolks, beaten
4 egg whites, beaten stiff
1 tablespoon vanilla
1 cup nuts, chopped

1) Heat 1 quart milk in double boiler, add one cup chopped dates, one cup raisins, and ½ cup currants. Scald milk and dried fruit mixture.

2) Dissolve 2 packages of Knox gelatin in one cup of cool water, let stand until milk is taken from stove.

3) In a separate bowl mix 4 tablespoons cocoa with 2 cups sugar. Add 4 beaten egg yolks and enough milk to give mixture pouring consistency. Stir batter into hot milk.

4) Cook several minutes, remove from stove and stir in dissolved gelatin. Cool until mixture starts to set, then add 1 cup whipped cream, 4 egg whites beaten stiff, 1 tablespoon vanilla and 1 cup chopped nuts.

Serves 8

K. Sprague
Sequim, WA

Three Layer Fruit Cake

3 cups plain flour
2 cups sugar
2 eggs
1 cup nuts
1 cup raisins
1 teaspoon vanilla
1 cup coconut
1 orange, chopped
½ cup butter
½ cup buttermilk
1 teaspoon soda
½ teaspoon salt
1 teaspoon allspice
1 cup strawberry jam
2 apples, chopped

Icing:
2 cups sugar
½ cup butter
1 to 2 cups raisins
1 teaspoon vanilla
1 cup Pet milk
2 cups coconut flakes
4 egg yolks
2 cups nuts
1 cup crushed pineapple

1) Sift together flour, soda, and salt. Set aside.

2) Beat together eggs, sugar, butter, allspice, jam, vanilla and buttermilk. Add nuts and dried fruit. Blend thoroughly. Pour into greased and floured cake pans. Bake at 325 degrees for 35 to 40 minutes.

3) Lightly beat egg yolks. Mix in milk and beat again, then add butter and vanilla. Put into a heavy saucepan. Cook until thick (about 10 minutes). Remove from heat, add the nuts and fruits. Cool and spread on the cake.

Serves 8

Lucille Davidson
Arb, AL

Classic Chocolate Ice Cream

7 ounces bittersweet chocolate, broken
1½ cups heavy cream
3 egg yolks
⅓ cup water
¼ cup sugar

1) Whip the cream in a chilled bowl until soft—not stiff. Set aside.

2) Beat the egg yolks until they appear to be the color of a lemon.

3) Dissolve the sugar in the water in a 6 cup pot on high heat. Let boil for 2-4 minutes (do not let water evaporate). Stir in the chocolate until it melts. The mixture should be extremely thick.

4) Add the hot chocolate to the egg yolks and beat until the mixture is smooth and thick. Stir until the mixture cools to room temperature.

5) Stir 2 tablespoons of the whipped cream into the room temperature chocolate. Stir in 3 more tablespoonfuls, one by one, until the chocolate's consistency matches that of the whipped cream. Fold in the chocolate to the remaining whipped cream.

6) Pour the ice cream into an ice cube tray, cover with foil and freeze for 2-4 hours until firm.

Makes 1 quart

Strawberry Brandy Cheese Cake

Crust:
3 cups crushed graham crackers
¼ cup sugar
½ cup melted butter or margarine

Filling:
1 cup sugar
4 eggs, beaten
1 teaspoon vanilla
5 tablespoons French brandy
½ teaspoon salt
3 (8 oz.) packages cream cheese
4 tablespoons plain flour
1 teaspoon vanilla flavoring
½ teaspoon salt
½ cup sour cream
¼ cup milk

Glaze
1 cup powdered sugar
1 teaspoon strawberrry flavoring
3 teaspoons French brandy

1) Mix cracker crumbs with sugar and melted butter. Press into bottom and sides of 10 inch spring form pan.

2) Cream the cheese. Add the sugar, blend well. Add beaten eggs and beat again. Add flour, salt, brandy, vanilla, sour cream, and milk. Beat well.

3) Pour into crust and bake at 450 degrees for 10 minutes. Reduce heat to 325 degrees and bake 1 hour. Turn oven off, open door and leave cake in oven until cool. Spread glaze on top of cake. Dot with whipped cream, if desired.

Serves 6

Lanie Jobe
Lenoir, NC

Peanut Butter Cups

1½ cups graham cracker crumbs
1 box (1 lb.) powdered sugar
1½ cups peanut butter
2 sticks margarine
1 package chocolate chips

1) Mix cracker crumbs with the powdered sugar. Melt peanut butter and 1½ sticks of the margarine together and combine with crumb mixture, making sure to work together well.

2) Spread in a 9 x 13 inch well greased pan packing down hard. Melt ½ stick margarine and chocolate chips until smooth. Spread over top of peanut butter mixture. When cooled and set, cut into squares.

Serves 10

Sandra Brookway
New Hope, AL

Caramel Layer Chocolate Squares

1 (14 oz.) package light caramels
⅔ cup evaporated milk
1 package German Chocolate cake mix
¾ cup margarine, melted
1 cup chocolate chips

1) Melt caramels and blend with ⅓ cup of the milk. Beat together cake mix, margarine and ⅓ cup of the milk.

2) Press half of cake mixture into greased 9 x 13 inch pan and bake for 6 minutes at 350 degrees. Spread chocolate chips over baked crust. Spread caramel mixture over chips, then rest of cake mixture.

3) Bake 15 to 18 minutes at 350 degrees. Cool and refrigerate to set caramels, then cut into squares.

Serves 8

Frank Cain, Sr.
Carroll, IA

White Chocolate Brownies

10 ounces white chocolate
4 ounces unsalted butter
4 eggs
2 cups sugar
1 teaspoon vanilla extract
1 cup flour, sifted
½ teaspoon salt
⅔ cup almonds, chopped

1) Butter and flour a 9 x 12 baking pan. Preheat oven to 325 degrees.

2) Grate 4 ounces of the chocolate. Melt remaining 6 ounces. Melt the butter.

3) Beat the eggs, sugar and vanilla until thick. Stir in the melted chocolate and the butter. Stir in the flour and the salt. Pour mixture into the buttered and floured baking pan.

4) Drop grated chocolate and almonds on top of the mixture and bake for 30 to 35 minutes. Let cool and serve.

Makes 1 dozen white brownies

Tea Party Nut Cups

Crust
3 oz. cream cheese
¼ lb. margarine
1 cup flour

Filling
¾ cup packed brown sugar
dash of salt
½ cup chopped pecans
1 teaspoon vanilla
1 tablespoon melted butter

1) Mix cream cheese and margarine together and blend in flour to make dough.

2) Divide crust into 24 balls; shape into cups. Fill with nut mixture and bake at 350 degrees until slightly brown.

Makes 24 balls

Mrs. Vivian A. Guy
North Webster, IN

Rich Chocolate
Sponge Cake Supreme

8 eggs
2 egg yolks
1 cup sugar
1½ teaspoons vanilla extract
1 cup flour, sifted
⅔ cup cocoa powder
¼ teaspoon salt
3 tablespoons unsalted butter, melted

1) Preheat oven to 350 degrees. Butter and flour a 10 inch baking pan.

2) Stir the eggs, sugar and vanilla over low heat until eggs are warm and sugar has melted. Beat for 10 minutes. The mix should end up extremely thick and larger in volume.

3) Sift the flour, cocoa and salt together. Fold in the dry mixture to the eggs in 3 separate portions. Quickly fold in the butter and then pour the batter into the buttered and floured pan.

4) Bake for 35 minutes. Let cool and serve with whipped cream.

Serves 12

Peach Ice Cream

4 cups milk
1¾ cups sugar
¾ teaspoon salt
1 teaspoon vanilla
4 cups heavy cream
4 cups ripe peaches, crushed

1) Heat 2 cups of the milk until luke warm. Add sugar and salt. Stir until dissolved. Add remaining milk.

2) Pour into ice cream can. Add vanilla and fold in lightly whipped cream. Chill in refrigerator for 30 minutes. Add crushed peaches to chilled mixture before churning. Churn and freeze according to instructions with machine.

Makes 4 quarts

Omar F. Gaylord
Adon, CA

Super-Duper Chocolate Drop Cookies

2 cups flour
½ teaspoon baking powder
¼ teaspoon baking soda
¼ teaspoon salt
½ cup unsalted soft butter
¾ cup brown sugar
1 egg
1½ teaspoons vanilla extract
3 ounces unsweetened chocolate, melted
⅔ cup milk
Chocolate frosting (see pg. 119)

1) Preheat your oven to 350 degrees.

2) Sift the flour, baking powder, baking soda and salt together.

3) Using an electric mixer at medium speed, mix the butter and the sugar in a large bowl until creamy.

4) Add in the egg and the vanilla, beating the mixture until it is fluffy. Then blend in the melted chocolate.

5) Place heaping tablespoonfuls of the mixture onto greased baking sheets, leaving about 2 inches between each cookie. Bake for 8 to 12 minutes, until they are firm to the touch. Remove and let cool.

Chocolate Frosting

1½ cups semisweet chocolate morsels
3 tablespoons unsalted butter
⅓ cup milk
3 cups sifted powdered sugar
1 tablespoon vanilla extract

1) Melt the chocolate morsels, butter and milk over simmering water until smooth.

2) Beat together with sugar and vanilla. Frost the cookies immediately and generously.

Makes two to three dozen cookies.

Rum Almond Torte

7½ ounces bittersweet chocolate, broken
¾ cup butter
4 eggs separated
¾ cup sugar, sifted
1½ tablespoons vanilla
¼ cup flour
½ cup almonds, ground
pinch cream of tartar
Rum Glaze (see pg. 121)

1) Melt chocolate and butter, stirring until smooth.

2) Beat egg yolks for 2 minutes while gradually adding ½ cup of sugar and vanilla. Beat into chocolate mixture.

3) Fold in flour and nuts.

4) Beat egg whites with cream of tartar until fluffy. Slowly add remaining ¼ cup of sugar, beating until stiff peaks have begun to rise.

5) Blend 1 egg white into chocolate mixture. Fold in remaining 3 egg whites.

6) Pour into 10 inch pan lined with parchment paper. Bake at 375 degrees for 30-35 minutes or until sides separate from pan. Let cool.

Rum Glaze

3½ ounces bittersweet chocolate, broken
5 tablespoons butter
1 tablespoon corn syrup
1½ tablespoon dark rum

1) Melt chocolate and butter, stirring until smooth.

2) Remove from heat. Stir in corn syrup and rum.

3) Spread a thin layer of the glaze over the top and sides of the cooled torte. Refrigerate for fifteen minutes or until the glaze is firm.

4) Reheat the remaining glaze until it is thin and pour over the chilled torte's top and sides. Let firm.

Serves 8-10

Chocolate Bavarian
Brandied Supreme

3 tablespoons water
1½ envelopes plain gelatin
2 cups milk
3 ounces unsweetened chocolate
1 cup sugar
6 egg yolks
1½ teaspoons vanilla extract
1½ tablespoons brandy
2 cups heavy cream

1) Pour water into a bowl and sprinkle in the gelatin. Put aside until it softens.

2) Heat the milk and chocolate together until the chocolate is completely melted. Remove from heat.

3) Beat the sugar, egg yolks and vanilla together until thick. Then add in the hot chocolate and milk, beating as you slowly pour.

4) Place the mixture on medium heat and stir constantly until it thickens. Do not let boil.

5) Take the mixture off of the heat and add the softened gelatin, stirring until it dissolves. Let stand until warm and then add in the brandy. Continue to let cool until the mixture is at room temperature and is about to gel.

6) Whip the cream until extremely thick but not stiff. Fold the cream into the mixture. Taste and add more brandy at this point if you so desire.

7) Pour mixture into an 8 cup mold and refrigerate overnight.

Serves 8-10

Marvelous Chocolate Mousse

17 ounces semisweet chocolate
2 cups heavy cream, well chilled
4 eggs, separated
2 eggs
2 tablespoons powdered sugar
2 tablespoons creme de cacao
1½ tablespoons vanilla extract

1) Melt the chocolate and let it cool until warm.

2) Whip the cream lightly until it forms average-stiff peaks.

3) Beat 4 egg yolks with 2 eggs for 4-5 minutes. Whisk the 4 egg whites until they begin to stiffen. Mix in the sugar and beat with the whisked egg whites until stiff peaks form.

4) Stir the cooled melted chocolate and two tablespoons of the whipped cream into the egg yolks. Continue to stir until the mixture is smooth, and then add in the remaining whipped cream.

5) Once the remaining cream is completely mixed in, add the creme de cacao and the vanilla, and then fold in the egg whites until the mixture is blended together.

6) Pour mousse into serving bowls and refrigerate overnight.

Serves 12

NOTES

NOTES

NOTES

NOTES

NOTES